PIANO SOLO

THE AMAZING SPIDER-MAN

MUSIC FROM THE MOTION PICTURE SOUNDTRACK
MUSIC COMPOSED BY JAMES HORNER

ISBN 978-1-4768-7158-5

HAL•LEONARD®
CORPORATION

7777 W. BLUEMOUND RD. P.O. BOX 13819 MILWAUKEE, WI 53213

In Australia Contact:
Hal Leonard Australia Pty. Ltd.
4 Lentara Court
Cheltenham, Victoria, 3192 Australia
Email: ausadmin@halleonard.com.au

Visit Hal Leonard Online at
www.halleonard.com

# MAIN TITLE - YOUNG PETER

By JAMES HORNER

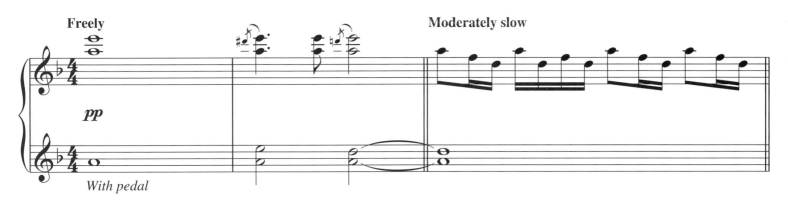

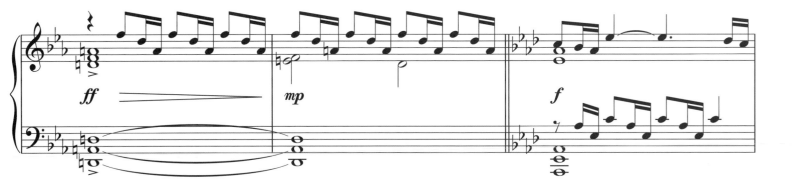

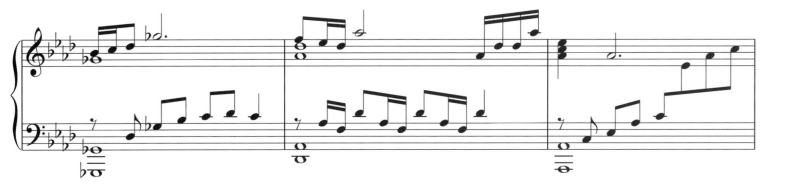

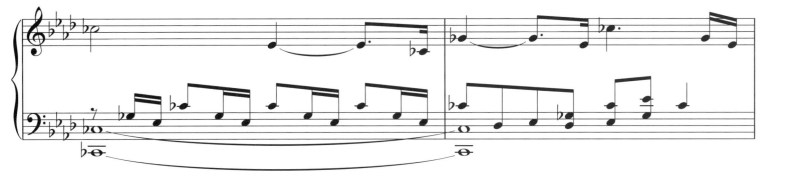

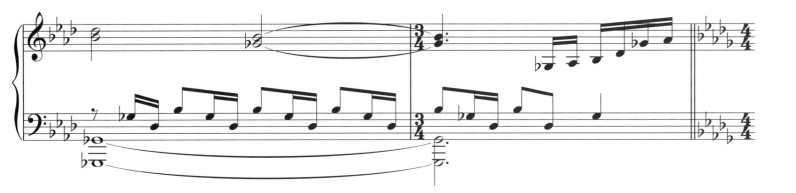

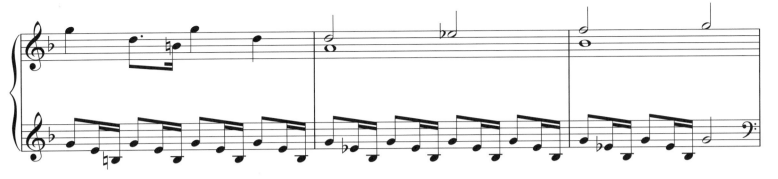

# BECOMING SPIDER-MAN

By James Horner

**Moderately fast**

*f*

*With pedal*

*sub.* **p**

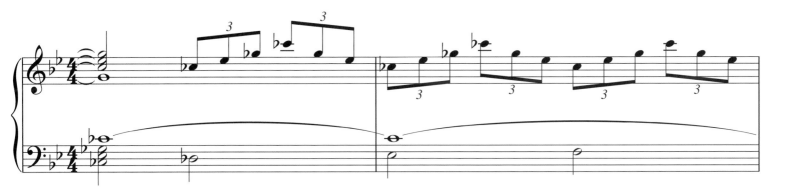

*cresc. poco a poco*

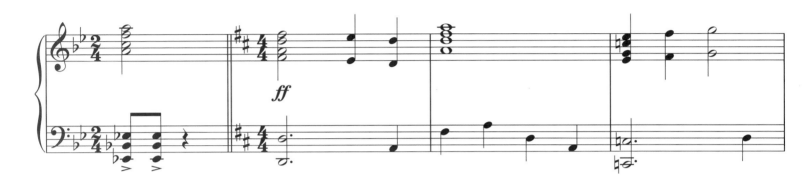

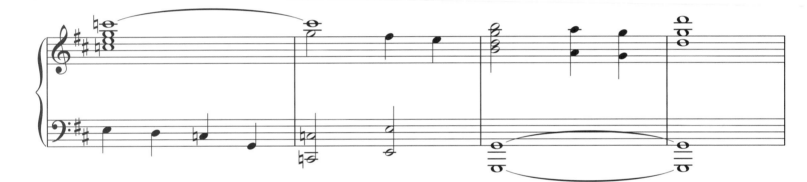

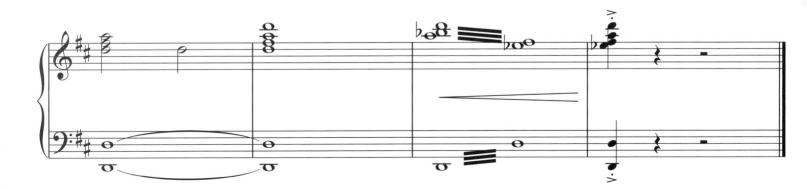

# PLAYING BASKETBALL

By JAMES HORNER

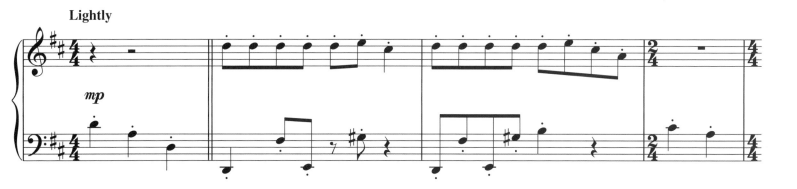

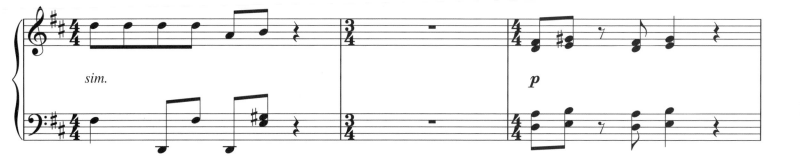

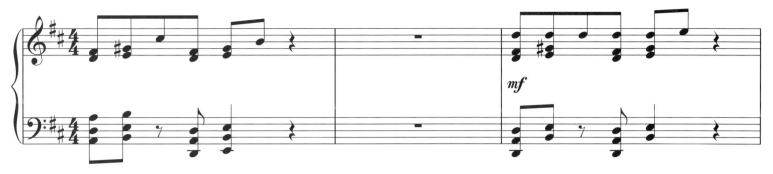

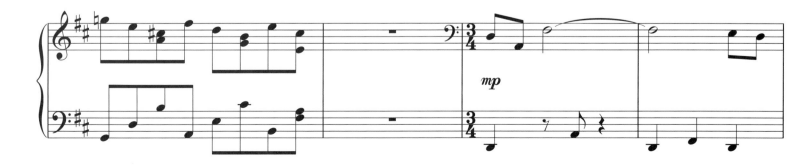

# THE BRIEFCASE

By JAMES HORNER

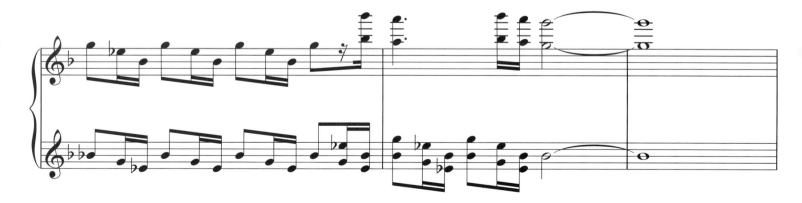

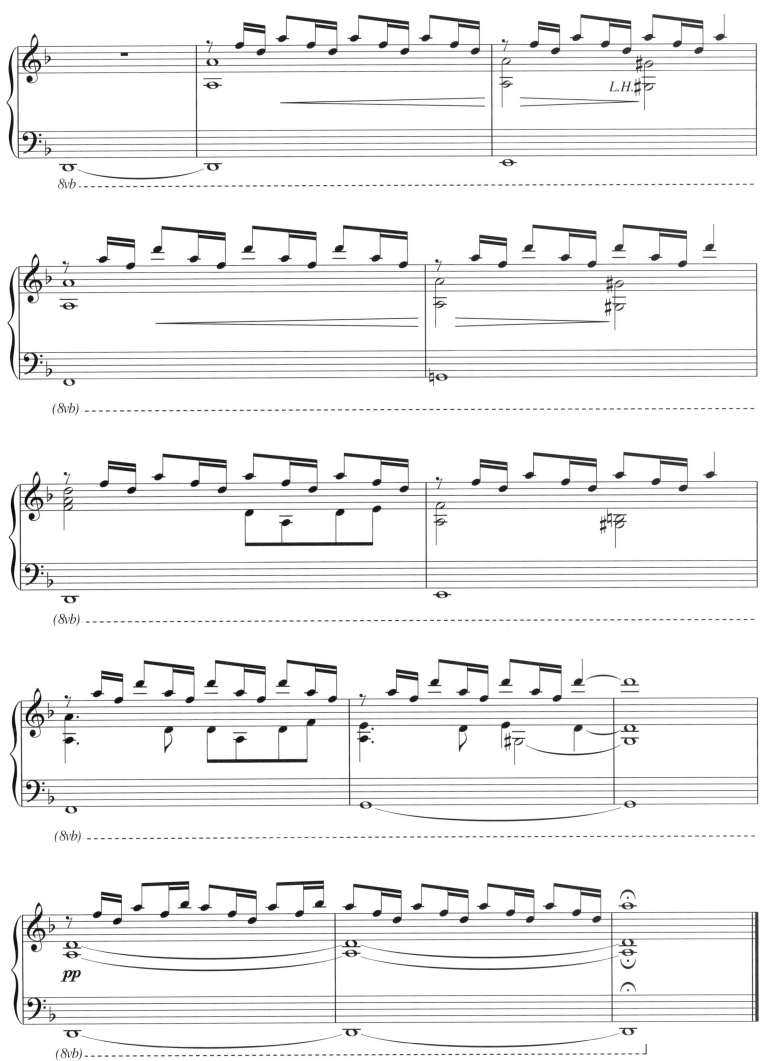

# THE SPIDER ROOM - RUMBLE IN THE SUBWAY

By JAMES HORNER

**Very slowly**

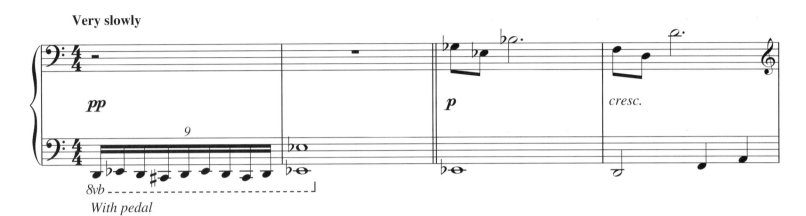

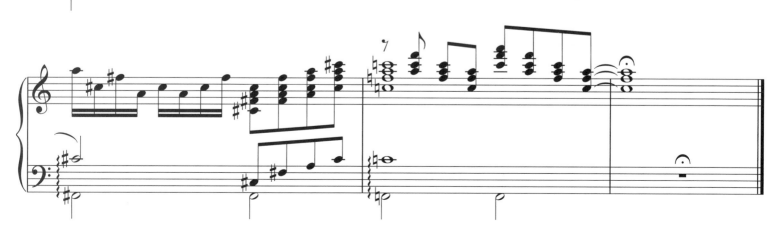

# SECRETS

By JAMES HORNER

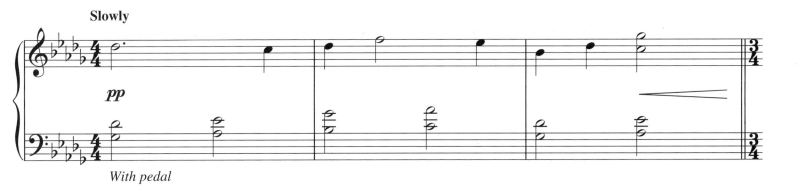

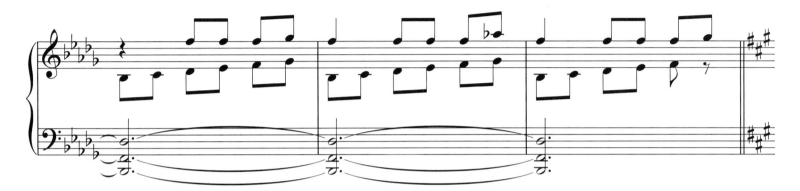

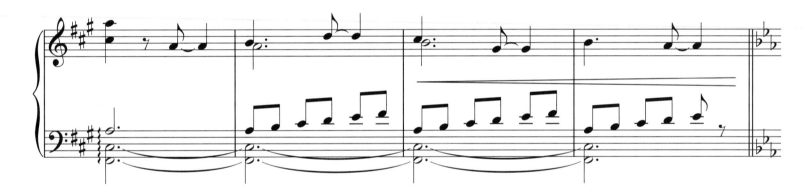

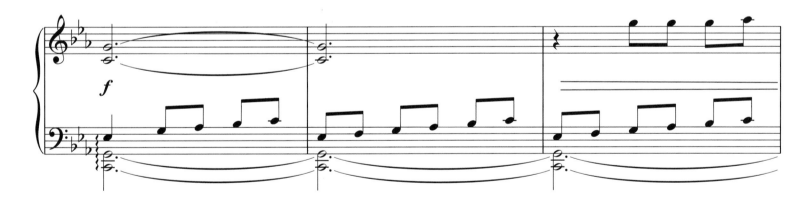

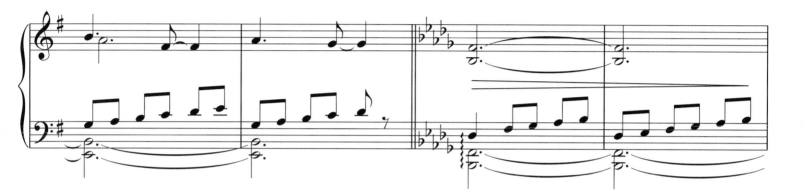

# METAMORPHOSIS

By JAMES HORNER

**Very slowly**

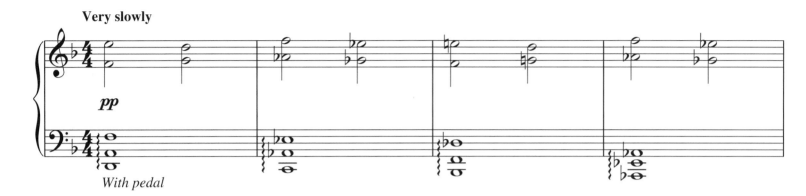

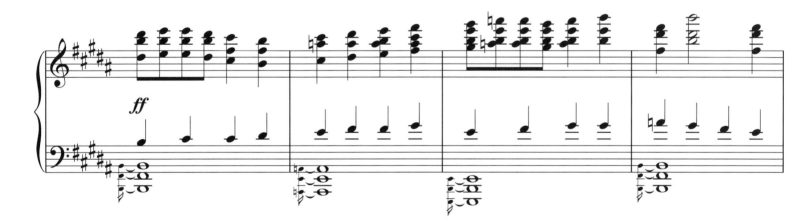

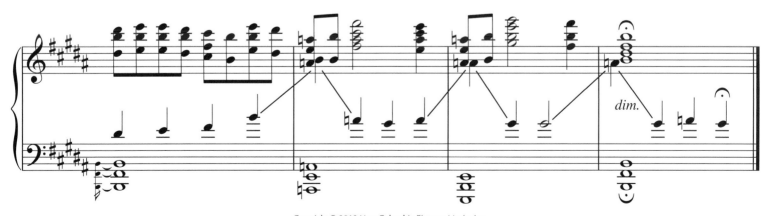

# ROOFTOP KISS

By JAMES HORNER

**Freely, with motion**

*With pedal*

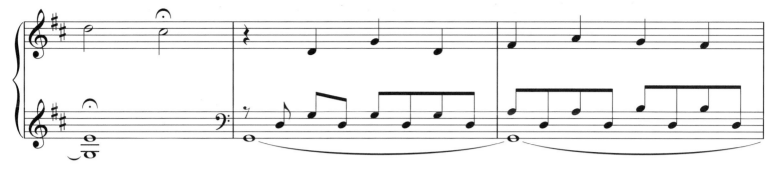

**Slower**

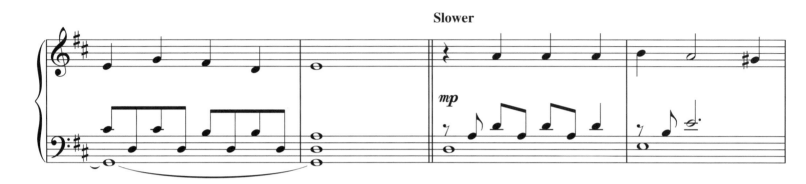

# I CAN'T SEE YOU ANYMORE

By JAMES HORNER

**Slowly**

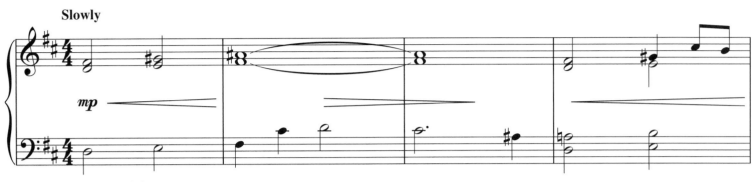

*With pedal*

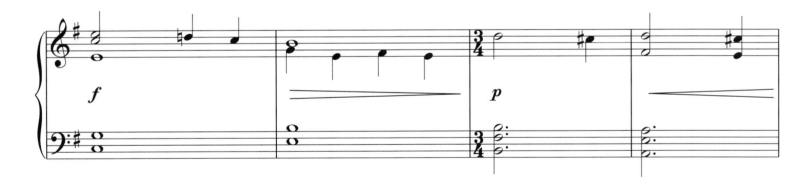

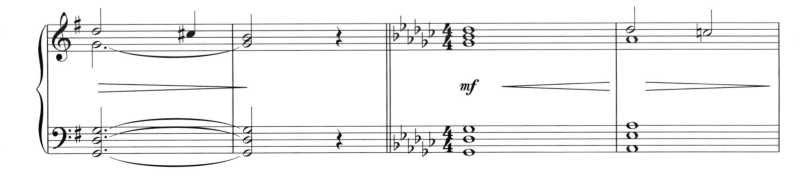

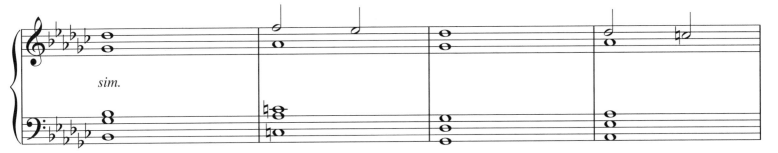

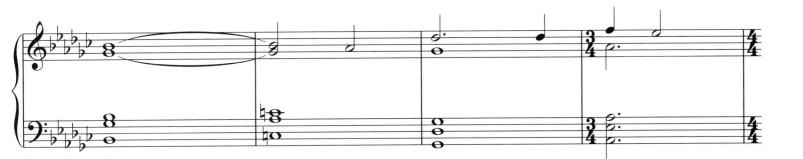

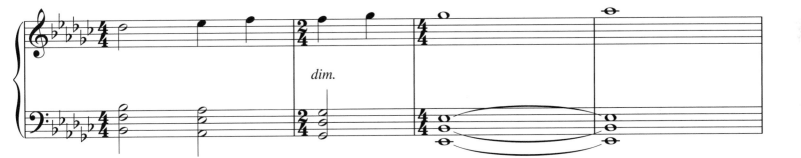

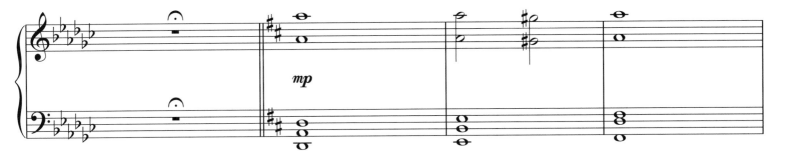

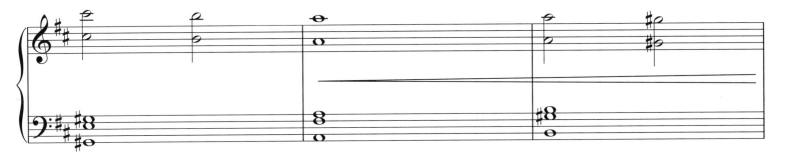

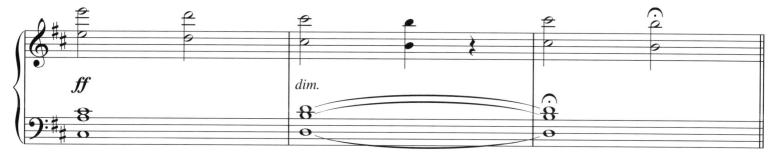

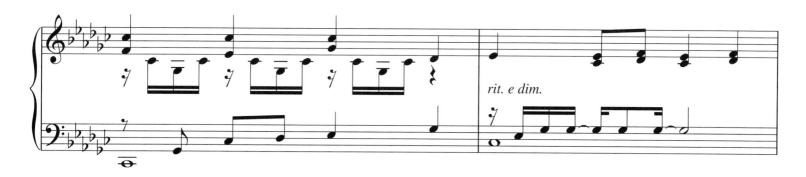

**Freely, with motion**

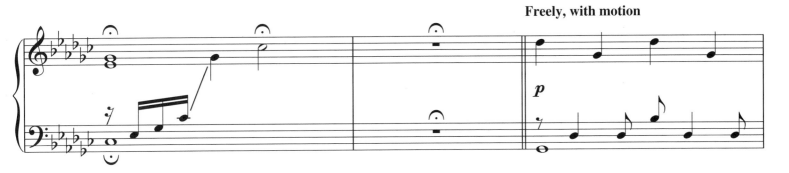

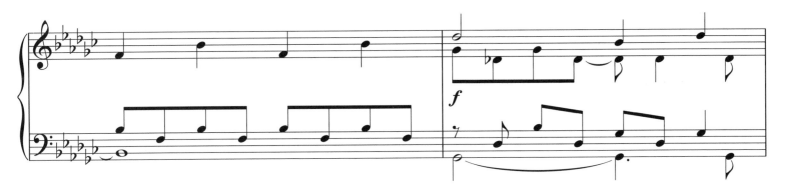

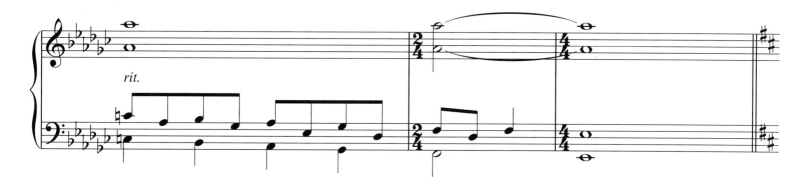

# PROMISES - SPIDER-MAN END TITLES

By JAMES HORNER

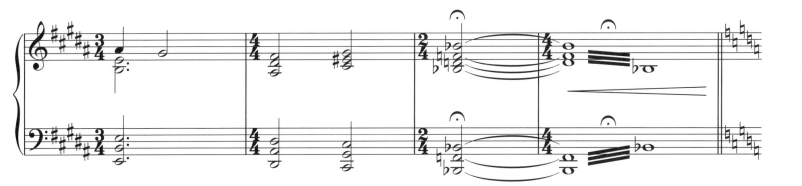

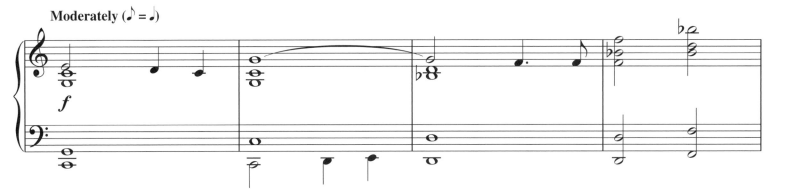

**Moderately** (♪ = ♩)

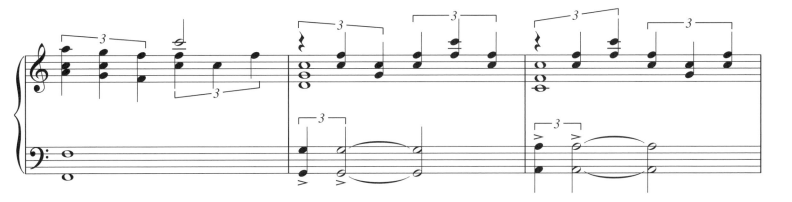

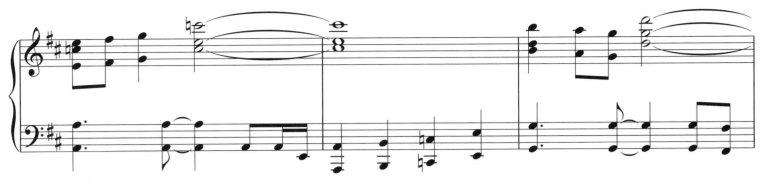

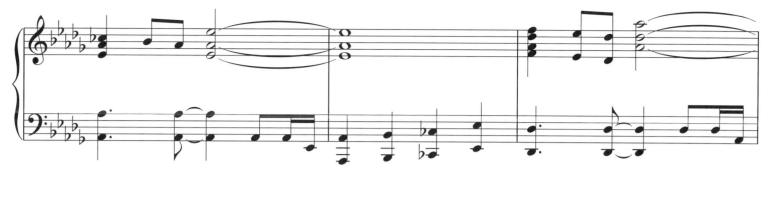

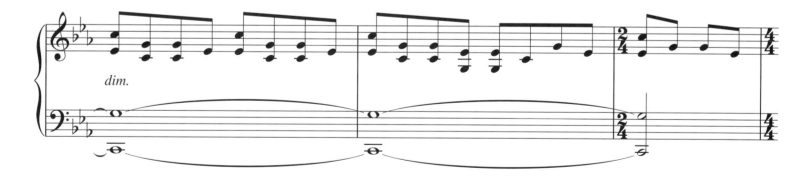

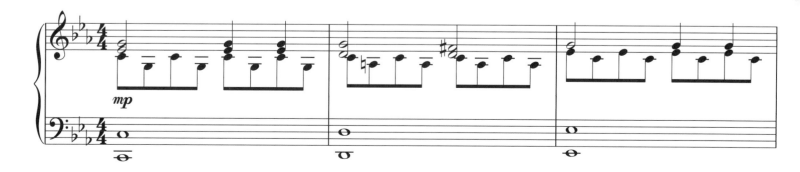

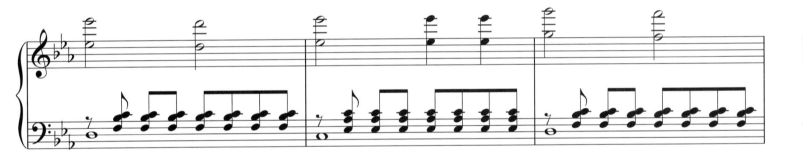

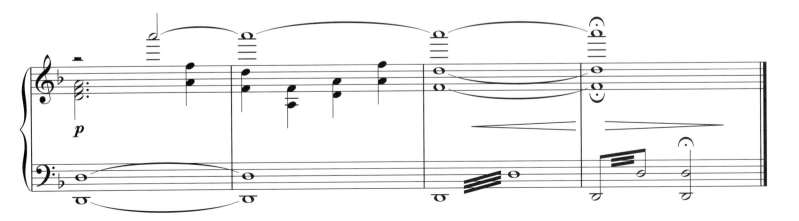